## Today's Top Drivers

# CHARLES LECLERC

### BY KATE MIKOLEY

**HOT TOPICS**

Gareth Stevens
PUBLISHING

Please visit our website, www.garethstevens.com. For a free color catalog of all our high-quality books, call toll free 1-800-542-2595 or fax 1-877-542-2596.

**Library of Congress Cataloging-in-Publication Data**
Names: Mikoley, Kate, author.
Title: Charles Leclerc / Kate Mikoley.
Description: Buffalo, New York : Gareth Stevens Publishing, [2024] | Series: Today's top drivers | Includes bibliographical references and index.
Identifiers: LCCN 2023009515 | ISBN 9781538287118 (library binding) | ISBN 9781538287101 (paperback) | ISBN 9781538287125 (ebook)
Subjects: LCSH: Leclerc, Charles, 1997–Juvenile literature. | FIA Formula One World Championship–Juvenile literature. | Automobile racing drivers–Monaco–Biography–Juvenile literature.
Classification: LCC GV1032.L44 M55 2024 | DDC 796.72092 [B]–dc23/eng/20230306
LC record available at https://lccn.loc.gov/2023009515
First Edition

Published in 2024 by
Gareth Stevens Publishing
2544 Clinton St
Buffalo, NY 14224

Copyright © 2024 Gareth Stevens Publishing

Designer: Tanya Dellaccio Keeney
Editor: Kate Mikoley

Photo credits: Series background Merydolla/Shutterstock.com; cover, p. 1 motorsports Photographer/Shutterstock.com; p. 4 Jens Mommens/Shutterstock.com; p. 5 FiledIMAGE/Shutterstock.com; p. 7 Kartpix Motorsport Archive/Alamy Images; p. 9 PHOTOMDP/Shutterstock.com; p. 11 LiveMedia/Shutterstock.com; p. 13 https://upload.wikimedia.org/wikipedia/commons/5/52/Charles_Leclerc_after_winning_F2_championship.jpg; p. 14 PatrickLauzon photographe/Shutterstock.com; pp. 15, 27 sbonsi/Shutterstock.com; p. 17 Michael Cola/Shutterstock.com; pp. 19, 21 cristiano barni/Shutterstock.com; pp. 23, 25 XPB Images Ltd/Alamy Images; p. 26 https://upload.wikimedia.org/wikipedia/commons/0/03/Jules_Bianchi_2012-1.JPG; p. 29 Jay Hirano Photography/Shutterstock.com.

All rights reserved. No part of this book may be reproduced in any form without permission in writing from the publisher, except by a reviewer.

Printed in the United States of America

Some of the images in this book illustrate individuals who are models. The depictions do not imply actual situations or events.

CPSIA compliance information: Batch #CS24GS: For further information contact Gareth Stevens, New York, New York at 1-800-542-2595.

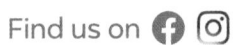

# CONTENTS

A Fast Formula................4
Meet Charles................6
Finding Ferrari................10
Fast in Formula 2................12
Formula 1 Fame................14
Driving into 2022................20
Family Ties................22
Racing for a Friend................24
Off the Track................26
Racing to the Future................28
Timeline................30
For More Information................31
Glossary................32
Index................32

# A FAST FORMULA

Formula 1 (F1) is a type of car racing with fans around the world. The cars have just one seat, open wheels, and an open cockpit, or driver's area. One of the most famous drivers in F1 today is Charles Leclerc.

## IN THE FAST LANE

The word "Formula" in Formula 1 means the rules of the sport. There is also Formula 2 and Formula 3 racing. Formula 1 is the top level of formula, or open-wheel, racing.

5

# MEET CHARLES

Charles Leclerc was born October 16, 1997, in the tiny country of Monaco. He got his start in racing at only 5 years old, when he started racing a kind of small race car called a kart or go-kart.

## IN THE FAST LANE

Many F1 stars got their start in kart racing. It's a way kids can get a hang of being behind the wheel.

7

As a kid, Leclerc won plenty of kart races, including the Monaco Kart Cup in 2010 and the Junior World Cup in 2011. By 2015, he started racing in Formula 3 races. In his first season, he was named best **rookie**.

## IN THE FAST LANE

*Leclerc finished in fourth place in the 2015 Formula 3 **championship**.*

# FINDING FERRARI

The car company Ferrari is a big name in F1 racing. In 2016, Leclerc joined the Ferrari Racing Academy, or training program. The academy, run by the Ferrari racing team, aims to help young drivers on their path to F1.

## IN THE FAST LANE

*In 2016, Leclerc won a set of races called the GP3 series.*

11

# FAST IN FORMULA 2

By 2017, Leclerc had made it to Formula 2 racing. That year, his car caught on fire during a race at the Silverstone Circuit, or track, in Great Britain. Even still, he went on to win the race!

# FORMULA 1 FAME

In 2018, Leclerc started racing in F1. He raced for the Alfa Romeo Sauber team. The next year, he signed with Ferrari. Many didn't think Leclerc was ready to race for a team as big as Ferrari, but he came in fourth in the World Championship.

## IN THE FAST LANE

After the 2019 season, Leclerc and Ferrari agreed he'd stay with the team through the 2024 season.

15

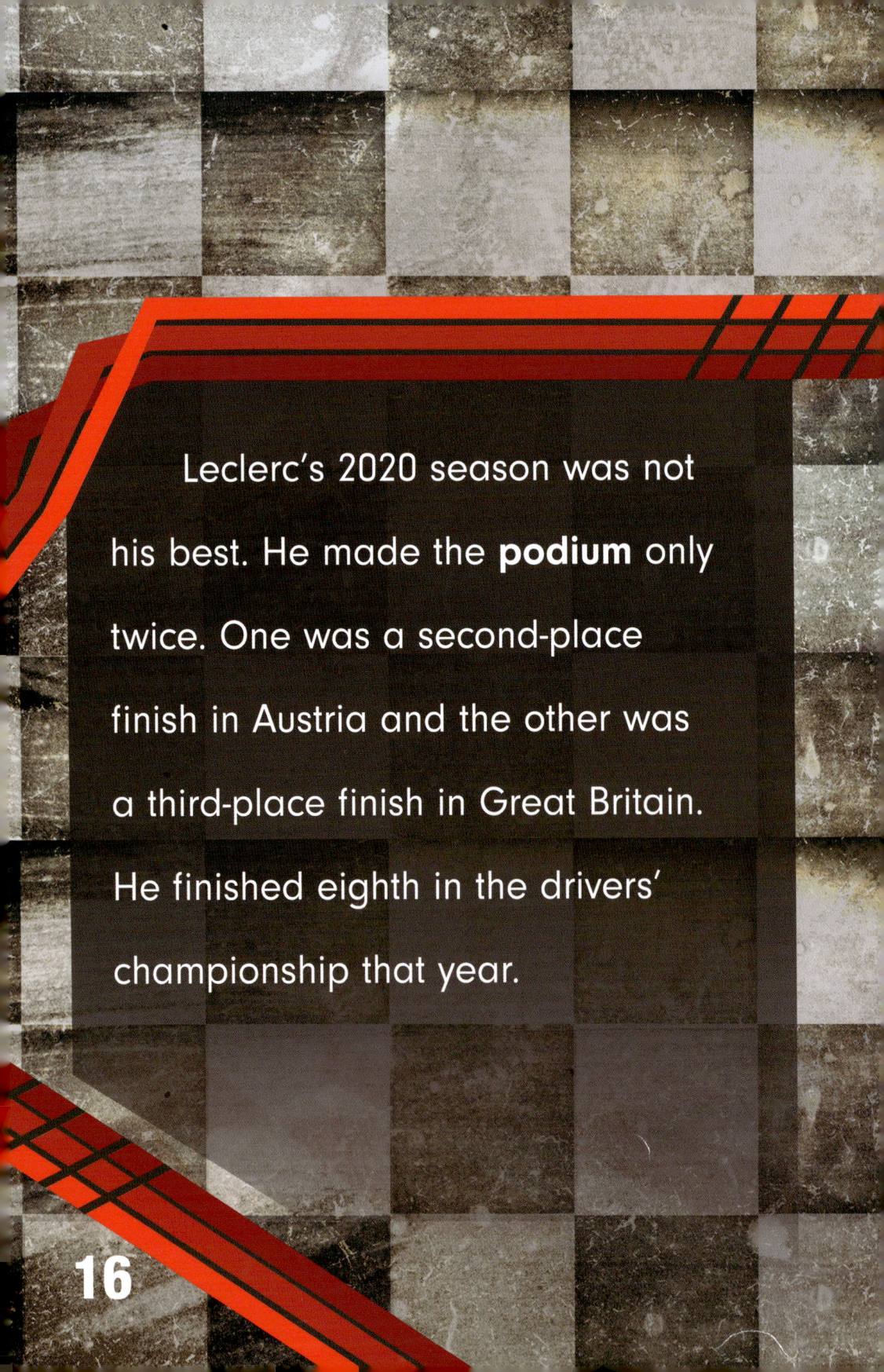

Leclerc's 2020 season was not his best. He made the **podium** only twice. One was a second-place finish in Austria and the other was a third-place finish in Great Britain. He finished eighth in the drivers' championship that year.

## IN THE FAST LANE

Even though he didn't win as much, Leclerc learned a lot in 2020. "Surely I'm a stronger driver than where I was at the beginning of the season," he said.

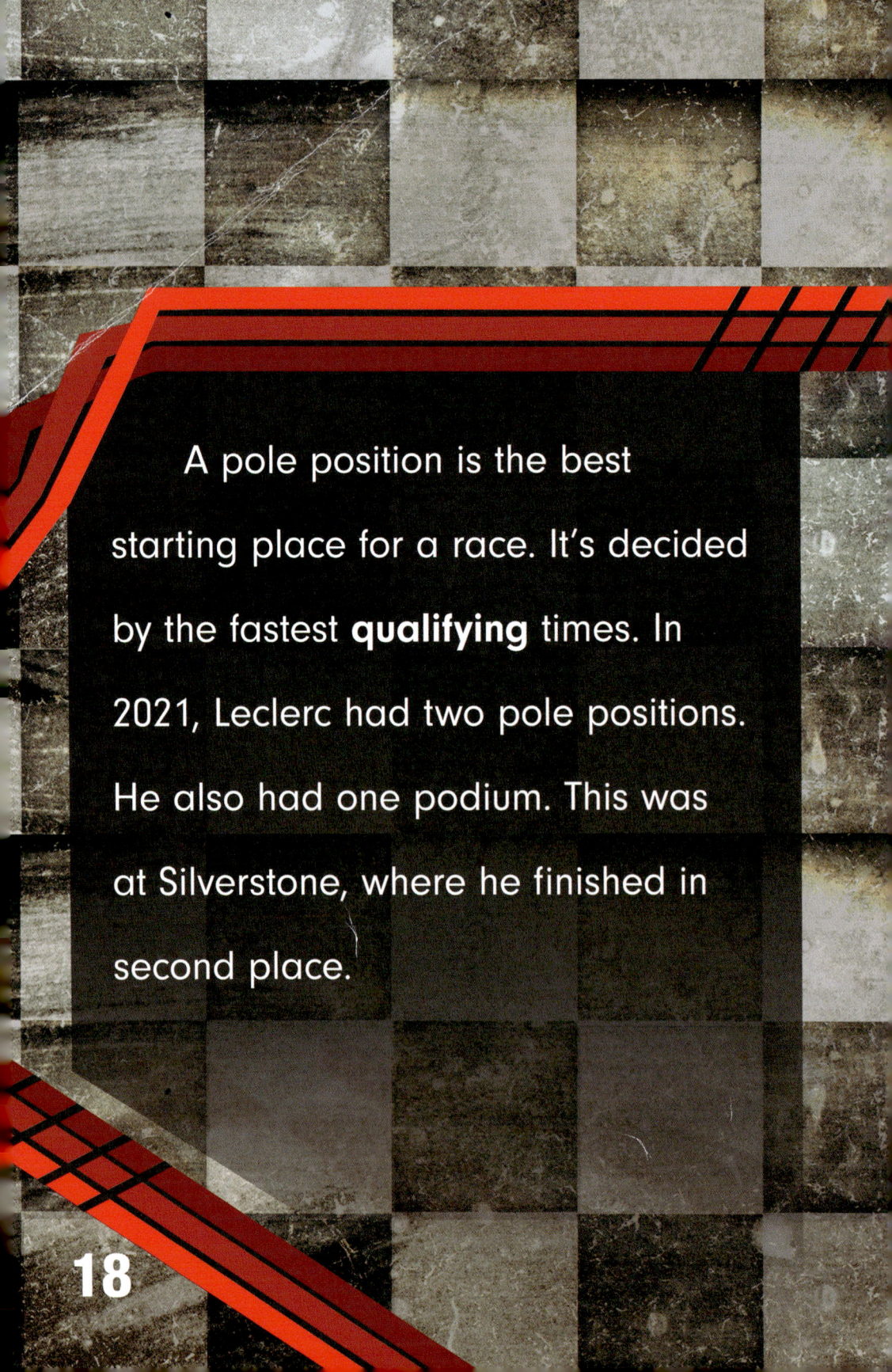

A pole position is the best starting place for a race. It's decided by the fastest **qualifying** times. In 2021, Leclerc had two pole positions. He also had one podium. This was at Silverstone, where he finished in second place.

## IN THE FAST LANE

Overall, Leclerc finished seventh in the 2021 drivers' championship. His driving helped Ferrari finish third in the **Constructors'** Championship.

19

# DRIVING INTO 2022

In the 2022 season, Leclerc showed the world what he was made of. He had nine pole positions, three wins, and five podium appearances. He came in second place overall, behind Max Verstappen who won in both 2021 and 2022.

## IN THE FAST LANE

**F1 races are held all over the world. Leclerc's 2022 wins were in the countries of Bahrain, Australia, and Austria.**

21

# FAMILY TIES

Charles is the middle child of Hervé and Pascale Leclerc. His father, Hervé, was a formula driver too. He raced in several Formula 3 races in the 1980s and 1990s. Hervé passed away in 2017.

**CHARLES AND HIS BROTHER, ARTHUR**

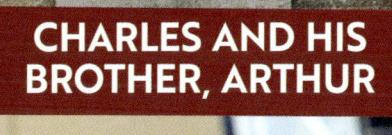

## IN THE FAST LANE

*Charles's older brother is named Lorenzo. His younger brother, Arthur, is a formula driver too.*

23

# RACING FOR A FRIEND

Charles Leclerc was good friends with F1 driver Jules Bianchi. He thought of Jules as a **mentor**. In 2015, Bianchi died as the result of a crash at the Japanese Grand Prix. Leclerc has said that without Bianchi, he would not be where he is today.

JULES BIANCHI

## IN THE FAST LANE

In the 2019 Monaco Grand Prix, Leclerc wore a special helmet. The left half looked like his father's helmet, while the right half matched Bianchi's.

25

# OFF THE TRACK

When he's not racing on the track, Leclerc can sometimes be found racing on the screen. He uses the video game **streaming** site Twitch. Thousands of fans have watched him play the official F1 video game and other racing games.

## IN THE FAST LANE

Leclerc also works with several **charities**, including the Princess Charlene Foundation. Named for the princess of Monaco, the charity helps lower the chances of drowning and teaches kids about sports.

27

# RACING TO THE FUTURE

What's next for a young racer whose driving seems to get better each season? Only time will tell! Known for being hard working and friendly, Leclerc seems ready to rule the world of Formula 1 racing!

## IN THE FAST LANE

Leclerc hasn't forgotten his start in karting. In 2019, he started his own line of karts!

29

# TIMELINE

**OCTOBER 16, 1997**
LECLERC IS BORN.

**2010**
HE WINS THE MONACO KART CUP.

**2011**
HE WINS THE JUNIOR WORLD CUP.

**2015**
LECLERC IS FOURTH IN THE FORMULA 3 CHAMPIONSHIP AND IS NAMED BEST ROOKIE.

**2016**
HE JOINS THE FERRARI RACING ACADEMY AND WINS THE GP3 SERIES.

**2017**
LECLERC WINS THE FORMULA 2 CHAMPIONSHIP.

**2018**
HE STARTS RACING IN F1.

**2019**
LECLERC JOINS THE FERRARI TEAM.

**2022**
LECLERC FINISHES SECOND IN THE DRIVERS' CHAMPIONSHIP.

# FOR MORE INFORMATION

## BOOKS

Albino, Dustin. *Superfast Formula 1 Racing.* Minneapolis, MN: Lerner Publications, 2020.

Gish, Ashley. *Formula One Cars.* Mankato, MN: Creative Education, 2021.

Rule, Heather. *GOATs of Auto Racing.* Minneapolis, MN: SportsZone, 2022.

## WEBSITES

**Charles Leclerc**
www.charlesleclerc.com/
Read a short profile and find out more about Leclerc on his official website.

**Charles Leclerc: F1 Driver Page**
www.formula1.com/en/drivers/charles-leclerc.html
Find Leclerc's latest stats on his F1 driver page.

**Official Driver: Charles Leclerc**
www.ferrari.com/en-EN/formula1/charles-leclerc
Ferrari's website has more information on Leclerc's life and racing stats.

**Publisher's note to educators and parents:** Our editors have carefully reviewed these websites to ensure that they are suitable for students. Many websites change frequently, however, and we cannot guarantee that a site's future contents will continue to meet our high standards of quality and educational value. Be advised that students should be closely supervised whenever they access the internet.

# GLOSSARY

**championship:** A contest to decide an overall winner.
**charity:** A group that helps those in need.
**constructor:** The person or group who builds something.
**mentor:** A person who provides advice and support to a less experienced person.
**podium:** A place where athletes get recognized when they come in first, second, or third place.
**qualifying:** Having to do with time trials that decide which drivers will be in the main race and what position they will start in.
**rookie:** A driver in their first year in a series.
**streaming:** Playing continuously as data is sent over the internet.

# INDEX

Bianchi, Jules, 24, 25
charity, 27
Ferrari, 10, 14, 15, 19
Formula 1, 4, 5, 7, 10, 14, 21, 24, 26, 28
Formula 2, 5, 12, 13
Formula 3, 5, 8, 9, 22
go-kart, 6, 7, 8, 29
Leclerc, Arthur, 23
Silverstone Circuit, 12, 18
Twitch, 27
Verstappen, Max, 20
video game, 26